Cy McCormick

Friend to Farmers

by Jordan Maxwell

SCHOOL PUBLISHERS

ISBN 10: 0-15-351427-2
ISBN 13: 978-0-15-351427-2

Ordering Options
ISBN 10: 0-15-351212-1 (Grade 2 Advanced Collection)
ISBN 13: 978-0-15-351212-4 (Grade 2 Advanced Collection)
ISBN 10: 0-15-358062-3 (package of 5)
ISBN 13: 978-0-15-358062-8 (package of 5)

Cyrus McCormick invented a machine called a reaper. Cyrus's reaper made it possible for farmers to cut and collect their crops faster than ever before. His reaper is still praised today.

This is the farm where Cyrus grew up.

Boyhood Dreams

Cyrus McCormick was born in 1809, and he grew up on his family's farm in Virginia. When he was a boy, Cyrus was very good at farming and inventing.

Cyrus dreamed of being able to earn money as an inventor. He was fifteen when he made his first invention. It was a cradle used for carrying grain, a type of seed.

These workers are using grain cradles.

Here farmers are cutting the grain crop by hand.

Making a Reaper

Cyrus's father had tried to build a machine pulled by horses to cut grain. He could never make it work properly. Cyrus decided to make his own machine, and he used his father's work as a starting point.

When Cyrus was young, farmers cut grain crops, such as wheat, by hand. They used a tool that looked like a big, curved knife. Harvesting was extremely difficult.

In 1831, Cyrus made a reaper that cut grain crops. The reaper also removed the hard outer shells of the grain. Cyrus's machine could cut the grain crop much faster than a person.

This is Cyrus McCormick's grain reaper.

Farmers came to see Cyrus's reaper, but they did not believe it would work. They thought it looked like a wheelbarrow, a carriage, and a flying machine! The farmers laughed at it and then returned home and kept using their old tools.

Cyrus did not give up, though. For
the next ten years, he did experiments to
improve his reaper. He even added a blade
that cut grain in wet weather.

Success!

In 1843, an inventor of another reaper challenged Cyrus to see whose machine would cut more grain. Luckily, it rained on the day of the contest. The other reaper jammed up, but Cyrus's machine kept working. That year, Cyrus sold twenty-nine reapers. He was on his way.

By 1847, Cyrus had so many orders for reapers that he could no longer store the supplies or make the machines at his farm workshop. He moved to a factory in Chicago. From there, he could provide enough machines to keep up with orders. By 1850, he was selling five thousand machines a year.

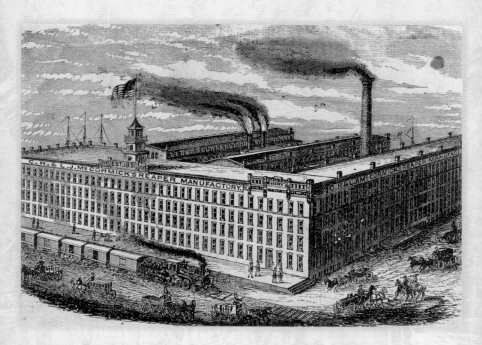

Cyrus McCormick's Chicago factory

World Famous

Soon Cyrus became famous all over the world. In 1851, Cyrus went to London. There, a committee gave him a special medal for his invention. In Europe, Cyrus was cheered for doing more for farming than any other living man.

When Cyrus came home, he faced some problems. Some people had tried to copy his invention. Then, the Chicago fire of 1871 destroyed his factory. Cyrus was determined to go on, and he rebuilt his factory.

The Chicago fire of 1871

A farmer using one of Cyrus McCormick's reapers

Cyrus died a rich man in 1884. His dream to earn money as an inventor came true. More importantly, Cyrus's reaper changed farming for generations to come.

Think Critically

1. What was Cyrus's first invention and how old was he when he invented it?

2. How do you think Cyrus felt when the farmers went home without believing his reaper would work?

3. In the book, where can you find information about when Cyrus first invented his reaper?

4. How did you feel when you read that Cyrus won a medal for his invention?

5. How did Cyrus make things better for farmers?

 **Social Studies**

Make a Time Line Using the information from the book, make a time line of Cyrus McCormick's life.

School-Home Connection Show a family member the picture of Cyrus's reaper on page 14. Talk about how it helped farmers. Then talk about inventions that have helped you.

Word Count: 557